MW01094716

Welcome to "Crystal Meaning Book: Unlocking the Mystical Powers: Guide cards to Gemstones Meanings" your comprehensive guide to the captivating world of crystals and gemstones. In this book, you'll embark on an enchanting journey of discovery as you explore the meanings, properties, and locations of 100 unique gemstones.

Each gemstone is showcased with its name and a stunning high-quality image, allowing you to appreciate the intricate details and vibrant colors of these precious stones. The white background provides a 4K realistic look, making each crystal come to life on the page.

Beyond visual beauty, you'll find succinct meanings that encapsulate the unique significance of each crystal, followed by short descriptions that uncover their properties and potential benefits. Affirmation quotes accompany each gem, offering you a direct channel to harness their energies.

As you delve deeper, you'll learn about the geographic locations where these gemstones are found, connecting you to the natural world in a profound way.

At the book's end, two indices—organized by crystal name and meaning—serve as handy references for quick navigation. Whether you're a seasoned crystal enthusiast or a curious newcomer, "Crystal Magic" is your portal to enlightenment, energy, and extraordinary beauty.

Turn the page and let the magic unfold.

Amethyst

Spiritual Growth and Protection

Amethyst is a powerful crystal known for its ability to enhance spiritual growth and provide protection. It helps to purify the mind, dispelling negative thoughts and aiding in meditation. Amethyst is also associated with sobriety and can support individuals in breaking addictive behaviors. Its calming energy promotes a sense of inner peace and balance.

"I am connected to my higher self, and I am protected by the divine energy of Amethyst."

Find locations: Brazil, Uruguay

Rose Quartz

Love and Compassion

Rose Quartz is the stone of love and compassion. It opens the heart chakra, promoting self-love, empathy, and deep emotional healing. It can enhance relationships, attract new love, and help in forgiving past hurts. Rose Quartz emits a gentle and soothing energy that creates an atmosphere of love and harmony.

"I am worthy of love, and my heart is open to give and receive it."

Find locations: Brazil, Madagascar, South Africa

Clear Quartz

Clarity and Amplification

Clear Quartz is a master healer crystal that amplifies energy and intentions. It enhances mental clarity, focus, and intuition. This versatile stone is used for various purposes, including meditation, balancing chakras, and promoting spiritual growth. Clear Quartz is like a blank canvas, allowing you to infuse it with your desired intentions.

"My mind is clear, my spirit is amplified, and my intentions are pure."

Find locations: Worldwide

Citrine

Abundance and Success

Citrine is a bright and joyful crystal associated with abundance and success. It helps to attract prosperity, wealth, and positive energies. Citrine is often used to manifest goals and dreams. It also radiates positivity and encourages a sunny disposition.

"I am a magnet for abundance, and success flows into my life effortlessly."

Find locations: Brazil, Madagascar, Russia

Lapis Lazuli

Wisdom and Truth

Lapis Lazuli is a stone of wisdom and truth, promoting self-awareness and inner peace. It enhances intellectual abilities and helps in understanding one's true self. Lapis Lazuli is also associated with communication and can aid in speaking your truth.

"I embrace my inner wisdom and communicate my truth with confidence."

Find locations: Afghanistan, Chile

5

Turquoise

Protection and Healing

Turquoise is a protective stone with powerful healing properties. It has been used for centuries for its ability to guard against negative energy and promote overall well-being. Turquoise is associated with enhancing communication and self-expression, making it valuable for public speaking and creative endeavors.

"I am surrounded by a protective shield, and my words flow with clarity and truth."

Find locations: USA, Iran, Mexico

Labradorite

Transformation and Magic

Labradorite is a stone of transformation and magic. It is known for its iridescent play of colors and is often used to awaken one's magical abilities. Labradorite can help you navigate through change and uncertainty, promoting inner strength and intuition.

"I embrace the magic within me, and I am open to transformation."

Find locations: Canada, Finland, Madagascar

Black Onyx

Protection and Grounding

Black Onyx is a protective and grounding crystal that absorbs and transmutes negative energy. It provides strength and support during challenging times and helps in making wise decisions. Black Onyx is associated with the root chakra, offering stability and a sense of security.

"I am grounded, protected, and empowered to face life's challenges."

Carnelian

Passion and Vitality

Carnelian is a vibrant crystal that enhances passion, creativity, and vitality. It stimulates the sacral chakra, promoting a zest for life and igniting the creative spark. Carnelian is also believed to attract success and prosperity.

"I am filled with passion and vitality, and I manifest my dreams with ease."

Find locations: Brazil, India, Madagascar

Moonstone

Intuition and Feminine Energy

Moonstone is a stone of intuition and feminine energy. It enhances psychic abilities, intuition, and inner balance. Moonstone is connected to the moon and is often used for fertility and emotional healing.

"I trust my intuition and embrace the cycles of life with grace."

Find locations: India, Sri Lanka, Australia

10

Hematite

Grounding and Protection

Hematite is a grounding stone that helps you stay connected to the Earth's energy. It provides a sense of stability and protection, making it an excellent choice for those who need to remain grounded. Hematite also enhances concentration and mental clarity.

"I am rooted in the present moment, and I am protected from negative energies."

Find locations: Brazil, Australia, Canada

Rhodonite

Emotional Healing and Compassion

Rhodonite is a powerful crystal for emotional healing and promoting compassion. It helps in releasing emotional pain and past wounds, allowing you to move forward with an open heart. Rhodonite also enhances self-love and encourages forgiveness.

"I release past pain and embrace the love and compassion within me."

Find locations: Russia, Sweden, Peru

Amazonite

Communication and Harmony

Amazonite is a stone of communication and harmony. It assists in expressing your thoughts and feelings with clarity and balance. Amazonite is also associated with soothing energies that promote a sense of calm and well-being.

"I communicate my truth with ease and embrace harmony in all aspects of my life."

Find locations: Brazil, United States, Madagascar   13

Malachite

Transformation and Protection

Malachite is a stone of transformation and protection. It is known for absorbing negative energies and helping you break free from old patterns. Malachite can stimulate personal growth and encourage positive transformation.

"I embrace change and protect my energy as I grow and transform."

Find locations: Democratic Republic of Congo, Zambia, Australia

14

Selenite

Cleansing and Clarity

Selenite is a cleansing crystal that clears and purifies energy. It is often used to cleanse other crystals and spaces. Selenite also enhances mental clarity and spiritual growth, connecting you to higher realms of consciousness.

"I am pure and clear, and my path is illuminated with divine clarity"

Find locations: Morocco, United States, Greece

Tiger's Eye

Courage and Confidence

Tiger's Eye is a powerful stone for courage and confidence. It helps you overcome fears and self-doubt, promoting a strong sense of self. Tiger's Eye also enhances willpower and decision-making.

"I am courageous, confident, and determined to achieve my goals."

Find locations: South Africa, Australia, United States

Fluorite

Mental Clarity and Focus

Fluorite is a crystal that enhances mental clarity and focus. It helps in organizing thoughts, making it an excellent aid for studying and problem-solving. Fluorite also cleanses and stabilizes the aura, promoting balance and harmony.

"My mind is clear and focused, and I approach challenges with ease."

Find locations: China, Mexico, United States

17

Pyrite

Abundance and Protection

Pyrite is often called "Fool's Gold" and is a stone of abundance and protection. It attracts prosperity and wealth while providing a shield against negative energies. Pyrite's energy is motivating and helps you take action toward your goals.

"I am abundant, protected, and guided by my inner wisdom."

Find locations: Spain, Peru, United States

Rhodochrosite

Love and Healing

Rhodochrosite is a crystal that encourages love and emotional healing. It opens the heart chakra, promoting self-love and compassion for others. Rhodochrosite also aids in releasing emotional pain and trauma.

"I am filled with love, and I heal from within with each breath."

Find locations: Argentina, South Africa, United States

Aquamarine

Calm and Courage

Aquamarine is a calming crystal that also promotes courage and self-expression. It's associated with the soothing energy of the ocean, bringing a sense of tranquility and clarity. Aquamarine encourages you to speak your truth and take courageous actions.

"I am calm, courageous, and I express myself with grace."

Find locations: Brazil, Madagascar, United States

Obsidian

Protection and Grounding

Obsidian is a powerful protective stone that absorbs and transforms negative energy. It provides a shield against psychic attacks and promotes emotional stability. Obsidian also enhances clarity and self-awareness.

"I am protected, grounded, and in control of my energy"

Find locations: Mexico, United States, Armenia

Aventurine

Luck and Abundance

Aventurine is a stone of luck and abundance. It brings good fortune and opportunities for prosperity. Aventurine is associated with the heart chakra, promoting emotional healing and balance. It is also a crystal of optimism and positive energy.

"I am open to the flow of abundance and embrace luck in every aspect of my life."

Find locations: India, Brazil, Russia

Smoky Quartz

Grounding and Protection

Smoky Quartz is a powerful grounding and protective crystal. It absorbs and transmutes negative energies, making it an excellent choice for spiritual protection. Smoky Quartz also enhances practicality and organization.

"I am grounded and protected, and I approach life with clarity and purpose."

Find locations: Brazil, United States, Switzerland

Garnet

Passion and Energy

Garnet is a stone of passion and energy. It helps you tap into your inner fire and vitality, enhancing your motivation and creativity. Garnet is associated with the root chakra, promoting a sense of security and strength.

"I am filled with passion and energy, and I pursue my goals with enthusiasm."

Find locations: India, Brazil, United States

24

Red Jasper

Nurturing and Grounding

Red Jasper is a nurturing and grounding crystal that provides stability and support. It helps in times of stress and promotes emotional healing. Red Jasper is associated with the root chakra, offering a sense of security and protection.

"I am nurtured and grounded, and I am strong in the face of challenges."

Find locations: United States, Brazil, India

Blue Lace Agate

Communication and Calm

Blue Lace Agate is a calming and soothing crystal that enhances communication and self-expression. It helps in speaking your truth with clarity and grace. Blue Lace Agate also promotes inner calm and relaxation.

"I communicate with ease, and my words are filled with peace and truth."

Find locations: Namibia, United States

Sunstone

Joy and Abundance

Sunstone is a joyful crystal associated with abundance and good fortune. It brings a sense of light and positivity into your life. Sunstone enhances self-worth and confidence, making it easier to manifest your desires.

"I am filled with joy, and abundance flows into my life effortlessly"

Find locations: United States, Norway, Canada

Amber

Healing and Protection

Amber is a fossilized tree resin with healing and protective properties. It provides a sense of warmth and well-being, aiding in physical and emotional healing. Amber is also associated with ancient wisdom and connection to the past.

"I am healed, protected, and connected to the wisdom of the ages."

Find locations: Baltic region, Russia, Dominican Republic 28

Kunzite

Unconditional Love

Kunzite is a crystal of unconditional love and emotional healing. It opens the heart to all forms of love and helps in releasing emotional pain. Kunzite also promotes inner peace and self-acceptance.

"I am surrounded by love, and I let go of all pain from the past."

Find locations: United States, Afghanistan, Brazil   29

Blue Apatite

Clarity and Focus

Blue Apatite is a crystal that enhances clarity and focus. It aids in setting and achieving goals, especially in the intellectual and creative realms. Blue Apatite also stimulates the throat chakra, promoting clear communication.

"I am clear, focused, and I express my ideas with precision"

Find locations: Brazil, United States, Mexico

30

Serpentine

Healing and Transformation

Serpentine is a crystal of healing and transformation. It assists in clearing blocked energy and provides support for personal growth and change. Serpentine is associated with the kundalini energy, helping it rise and activate.

"I am healed and transformed, and I embrace the flow of life."

Find locations: United States, Canada, Afghanistan

Howlite

Calm and Awareness

Howlite is a calming crystal that enhances awareness and mindfulness. It helps to reduce stress and promote a sense of inner peace. Howlite is often used for meditation and sleep improvement.

"I am calm, aware, and at peace in every moment."

Find locations: United States, Canada, Mexico

Rhodolite Garnet

Love and Passion

Rhodolite Garnet is a crystal of love and passion. It enhances sensuality, self-confidence, and emotional healing. Rhodolite Garnet is associated with the heart chakra, promoting love and connection.

"I am passionate, confident, and open to love in all its forms."

Find locations: India, United States, Brazil

Blue Topaz

Communication and Truth

Blue Topaz is a crystal that enhances communication and truth. It helps in expressing thoughts and feelings with clarity and precision. Blue Topaz is also associated with emotional healing and balance.

"I communicate with honesty and clarity, and I embrace emotional harmony."

Find locations: Brazil, United States, Mexico

Chrysocolla

Communication and Calm

Chrysocolla is a calming and soothing crystal that enhances communication and self-expression. It helps in speaking your truth with clarity and grace. Chrysocolla also promotes inner calm and relaxation.

"I communicate with ease, and my words are filled with peace and truth."

Find locations: United States, Peru, Chile

Blue Calcite

Communication and Relaxation

Blue Calcite is a crystal that enhances communication and relaxation. It helps you express your thoughts and feelings with ease. Blue Calcite also promotes inner peace and emotional healing.

"I communicate with relaxation and ease, and I am at peace in every moment."

Find locations: Mexico, United States

Green Aventurine

Luck and Prosperity

Green Aventurine is a crystal of luck and prosperity. It brings good fortune and opportunities for financial growth. Green Aventurine is associated with the heart chakra, promoting emotional healing and balance.

"I am open to the flow of prosperity and embrace luck in every aspect of my life."

Find locations: India, Brazil, Russia

Prehnite

Calm and Inner Knowing

Prehnite is a calming crystal that enhances inner knowing and spiritual growth. It helps you connect with your intuition and guides you in making the right decisions. Prehnite is often used for dreamwork and meditation.

"I am calm, intuitive, and in tune with my inner wisdom."

Find locations: South Africa, Australia, China

Rutilated Quartz

Energy and Amplification

Rutilated Quartz is a crystal of energy and amplification. It contains golden rutile inclusions that enhance energy flow and intentions. Rutilated Quartz is often used for manifesting and increasing personal power.

"I am filled with energy and my intentions are amplified for the highest good"

Find locations: Brazil, United States, Madagascar

Blue Kyanite

Communication and Alignment

Blue Kyanite is a crystal that enhances communication and energetic alignment. It helps you connect with your higher self and express your truth. Blue Kyanite is also a powerful crystal for chakra balancing and energy clearing.

"I am aligned with my higher self, and I communicate with clarity and purpose."

Find locations: Brazil, India, Switzerland

Angelite

Angelic Connection and Peace

Angelite is a crystal that enhances connection with angelic realms and promotes inner peace. It brings a sense of calm and tranquility, making it valuable for meditation and spiritual growth. Angelite also supports clear communication with the divine.

"I am connected to the angels, and I am at peace with the universe."

Find locations: Peru, Mexico, Germany

Dumortierite

Patience and Clarity

Dumortierite is a crystal that enhances patience and mental clarity. It helps in overcoming obstacles and promoting a sense of mental discipline. Dumortierite is associated with the throat chakra, aiding in clear communication.

"I am patient, clear, and I overcome challenges with grace."

Find locations: Brazil, France, Poland

Ruby

Passion and Vitality

Ruby is a crystal of passion and vitality. It enhances love, self-confidence, and physical energy. Ruby is associated with the root chakra, promoting a sense of security and strength.

"I am filled with passion and vitality, and I live life with enthusiasm."

Find locations: Myanmar, Thailand, Sri Lanka

Peridot

Abundance and Growth

Peridot is a crystal associated with abundance and personal growth. It attracts prosperity and helps you manifest your desires. Peridot is also a stone of transformation and rebirth.

"I am abundant, and I embrace personal growth and transformation."

Find locations: Pakistan, Egypt, United States

Azurite

Psychic Awareness and Inner Wisdom

Azurite is a crystal that enhances psychic awareness and inner wisdom. It helps you access higher states of consciousness and gain insights from your higher self. Azurite is often used for meditation and spiritual development.

"I am in tune with my psychic abilities, and I access inner wisdom with ease."

Find locations: Australia, Morocco, United States   46

Green Calcite

Heart Healing and Renewal

Green Calcite is a crystal of heart healing and renewal. It helps in releasing old emotional patterns and promotes a sense of emotional balance. Green Calcite is associated with the heart chakra, supporting love and compassion.

"I release old wounds and embrace love and renewal in my heart."

Find locations: Mexico, United States, Brazil

Blue Chalcedony

Communication and Harmony

Blue Chalcedony is a crystal that enhances communication and harmony. It helps in expressing thoughts and feelings with clarity and balance. Blue Chalcedony also promotes a sense of calm and well-being.

"I communicate my truth with ease, and I embrace harmony in all aspects of my life."

Find locations: United States, Brazil, Namibia

Iolite

Intuition and Inner Vision

Iolite is a crystal of intuition and inner vision. It enhances psychic abilities and helps you access deeper insights. Iolite is often used for journeying within and exploring one's inner world.

"I trust my intuition and embrace my inner vision with clarity"

Find locations: India, Brazil, Sri Lanka

Red Carnelian

Motivation and Creativity

Red Carnelian is a crystal of motivation and creativity. It stimulates the sacral chakra, enhancing passion and vitality. Red Carnelian is a powerful crystal for setting and achieving goals.

"I am motivated, creative, and I manifest my desires with enthusiasm."

Find locations: Brazil, India, United States

Blue Sodalite

Communication and Insight

Blue Sodalite is a crystal that enhances communication and inner insight. It helps in expressing thoughts and feelings with clarity and promotes self-awareness. Blue Sodalite is also associated with logical thinking and problem-solving.

"I communicate with insight and clarity, and I am self-aware."

Find locations: Brazil, Canada, India

Green Jade

Abundance and Harmony

Green Jade is a crystal associated with abundance and harmony. It brings good luck and prosperity while promoting emotional balance. Green Jade is also a symbol of purity and serenity.

"I am open to abundance and harmony in all aspects of my life."

Find locations: China, Myanmar, United States

Charoite

Transformation and Spirituality

Charoite is a crystal of transformation and spirituality. It aids in releasing old patterns and embracing personal growth. Charoite also enhances spiritual insight and connection.

"I am transformed and in tune with my spiritual self."

Find locations: Russia

Green Tourmaline

Healing and Protection

Green Tourmaline is a crystal of healing and protection. It helps in healing the heart and promoting a sense of security. Green Tourmaline is also associated with emotional balance and well-being.

"I am healed and protected, and my heart is in balance."

Find locations: Brazil, Afghanistan, United States

Chrysoprase

Heart Healing and Love

Chrysoprase is a crystal of heart healing and love. It opens the heart chakra, promoting self-love and compassion for others. Chrysoprase also enhances joy and happiness.

"I am filled with love and joy, and my heart is open to all forms of love."

Find locations: Australia, Brazil, United States

Blue Celestite

Angelic Connection and Peace

Blue Celestite is a crystal that enhances connection with angelic realms and promotes inner peace. It brings a sense of calm and tranquility, making it valuable for meditation and spiritual growth. Blue Celestite also supports clear communication with the divine.

"I am connected to the angels, and I am at peace with the universe."

Find locations: Madagascar, United States, Egypt

Lepidolite

Calm and Stress Relief

Lepidolite is a calming crystal that promotes inner peace and stress relief. It contains lithium, which helps reduce anxiety and bring a sense of tranquility. Lepidolite is often used for emotional healing and balance.

"I am calm, at peace, and stress-free in every moment."

Find locations: United States, Brazil, Russia

Green Malachite

Transformation and Protection

Malachite is a stone of transformation and protection. It is known for absorbing negative energies and helping you break free from old patterns. Malachite can stimulate personal growth and encourage positive transformation.

"I embrace change and protect my energy as I grow and transform."

Find locations: Democratic Republic of Congo, Zambia, Australia

Chalcopyrite

Abundance and Manifestation

Chalcopyrite is a crystal associated with abundance and manifestation. It helps in attracting prosperity and opportunities for success. Chalcopyrite is often used for setting and achieving goals.

"I am a magnet for abundance, and my manifestations come to life."

Find locations: Peru, China, Mexico

Snowflake Obsidian

Protection and Balance

Snowflake Obsidian is a protective crystal that promotes balance and inner harmony. It helps in releasing old patterns and negative energies. Snowflake Obsidian is often used for meditation and grounding.

"I am protected, balanced, and free from negative influences."

Find locations: United States, Mexico, Armenia

Peacock Ore

Creativity and Joy

Peacock Ore, also known as Bornite, is a crystal associated with creativity and joy. It brings a sense of color and energy to your life. Peacock Ore is often used for chakra balancing and inner transformation.

"I am creative and filled with joy, and my life is a colorful masterpiece."

Find locations: United States

Blue Lepidolite

Emotional Healing and Calm

Blue Lepidolite is a calming crystal that promotes emotional healing and a sense of calm. It contains lithium, which helps reduce anxiety and bring tranquility. Blue Lepidolite is often used for stress relief and relaxation.

"I am emotionally healed, calm, and stress-free in every moment."

Find locations: United States

Red Garnet

Passion and Energy

Red Garnet is a stone of passion and energy. It helps you tap into your inner fire and vitality, enhancing your motivation and creativity. Garnet is associated with the root chakra, promoting a sense of security and strength.

"I am filled with passion and energy, and I pursue my goals with enthusiasm."

Find locations: India, Brazil, United States

Blue Chrysocolla

Communication and Calm

Blue Chrysocolla is a calming and soothing crystal that enhances communication and self-expression. It helps in speaking your truth with clarity and grace. Blue Chrysocolla also promotes inner calm and relaxation.

"I communicate with ease, and my words are filled with peace and truth"

Find locations: Peru, United States, Chile

Red Coral

Passion and Protection

Red Coral is a crystal of passion and protection. It is often used in jewelry and amulets to enhance vitality and ward off negativity. Red Coral is associated with the root chakra, promoting physical and emotional protection.

"I am filled with passion and protected from harm in every aspect of my life."

Find locations: Italy, Japan, Australia

Blue Tiger's Eye

Insight and Clarity

Blue Tiger's Eye is a crystal that enhances insight and clarity. It helps you see the truth in situations and promotes mental focus. Blue Tiger's Eye is often used for grounding and protection.

"I am in tune with my intuition, and my mind is clear and focused."

Find locations: South Africa, United States, Australia

Green Serpentine

Healing and Transformation

Green Serpentine is a crystal of healing and transformation. It assists in clearing blocked energy and provides support for personal growth and change. Green Serpentine is associated with the kundalini energy, helping it rise and activate.

"I am healed and transformed, and I embrace the flow of life."

Find locations: United States, Canada, Afghanistan

Moldavite

Transformation and Spiritual Growth

Moldavite is a crystal of transformation and spiritual growth. It is believed to be of extraterrestrial origin and has a powerful, high-vibrational energy. Moldavite accelerates personal growth and spiritual awakening.

"I am transformed and connected to the higher realms of consciousness."

Find locations: Czech Republic

69

Angel Aura Quartz

Angelic Connection and Harmony

Angel Aura Quartz is a crystal that enhances connection with angelic realms and promotes inner harmony. It has a beautiful iridescent sheen that radiates a sense of peace and tranquility. Angel Aura Quartz is often used for meditation and spiritual growth.

"I am connected to the angels, and I embrace harmony in all aspects of my life."

Find locations: United States, Brazil

Lemurian Quartz

Spiritual Growth and Connection

Lemurian Quartz is a crystal associated with spiritual growth and connection. It is believed to hold the wisdom of ancient Lemuria and promotes deep inner healing. Lemurian Quartz also enhances communication with higher realms.

"I am on a path of spiritual growth and deep inner healing"

Find locations: Brazil, Madagascar

Unakite

Emotional Healing and Balance

Unakite is a crystal for emotional healing and balance. It promotes harmony in relationships and inner peace. Unakite also aids in releasing old emotional patterns and achieving emotional well-being.

"I am emotionally healed, and I embrace balance and harmony in my life."

Find locations: United States, South Africa, Brazil

Blue Azurite

Psychic Awareness and Inner Wisdom

Blue Azurite is a crystal that enhances psychic awareness and inner wisdom. It helps you access higher states of consciousness and gain insights from your higher self. Blue Azurite is often used for meditation and spiritual development.

"I am in tune with my psychic abilities, and I access inner wisdom with ease."

Find locations: Australia, Morocco, United States

Green Apatite

Clarity and Manifestation

Green Apatite is a crystal that enhances clarity and manifestation. It aids in setting and achieving goals, especially in the intellectual and creative realms. Green Apatite also stimulates the throat chakra, promoting clear communication.

"I am clear, focused, and I express my ideas with precision."

Find locations: Brazil, United States, Mexico

Petrified Wood

Grounding and Transformation

Petrified Wood is a crystal of grounding and transformation. It is fossilized wood that carries the energy of ancient trees. Petrified Wood enhances stability, support, and personal growth.

"I am grounded and supported, and I embrace transformation in my life."

Find locations: United States, Argentina, Madagascar

Blue Larimar

Calm and Communication

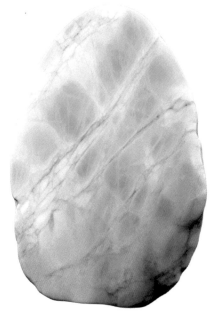

Blue Larimar is a calming crystal that enhances communication and inner peace. It is often associated with the energies of the ocean, promoting serenity and relaxation. Blue Larimar also supports clear communication.

"I communicate with calm and ease, and my words are filled with peace."

Find locations: Dominican Republic

Ruby Fuchsite

Heart Healing and Love

Ruby Fuchsite is a crystal of heart healing and love. It combines the energies of Ruby and Fuchsite, promoting self-love, compassion, and emotional healing. Ruby Fuchsite also enhances joy and happiness.

"I am filled with love and joy, and my heart is open to all forms of love."

Find locations: India, Brazil, United States

Chiastolite

Protection and Balance

Chiastolite, also known as the Cross Stone, is a crystal that offers protection and balance. It is known for its distinctive cross pattern and is often used as an amulet for spiritual protection. Chiastolite also enhances a sense of balance and inner harmony.

"I am protected and balanced in all aspects of my life."

Find locations: Spain, China, United States

Pietersite

Transformation and Clarity

Pietersite is a crystal of transformation and clarity. It helps in releasing old patterns and promoting mental focus. Pietersite is often associated with the higher self and spiritual growth.

"I am transformed, and my mind is clear and focused on my path of growth."

Find locations: Namibia, China, United States

Blue Aventurine

Calm and Insight

Blue Aventurine is a calming crystal that enhances insight and inner peace. It helps you connect with your intuition and promotes mental clarity. Blue Aventurine is often used for relaxation and stress relief.

"I am calm, intuitive, and my mind is clear and focused."

Find locations: Brazil, India, United States

Bismuth

Transformation and Creativity

Bismuth is a crystal of transformation and creativity. It forms unique, colorful geometric structures and enhances creativity, especially in the realm of the arts. Bismuth also promotes personal growth and change.

"I am transformed and creative, and I embrace change with grace."

Find locations: Canada, Germany, Peru

Botswana Agate

Balance and Protection

Botswana Agate is a crystal that promotes balance and protection. It enhances emotional stability and helps in times of stress. Botswana Agate also encourages a sense of security and inner harmony.

"I am balanced and protected, and I navigate life's challenges with ease."

Find locations: Botswana

Blue Goldstone

Ambition and Confidence

Blue Goldstone is a crystal that enhances ambition and confidence. It is often used to achieve goals and boost self-esteem. Blue Goldstone also promotes positivity and vitality.

"I am ambitious, confident, and I manifest success with enthusiasm."

Find locations: Italy, Germany, United States

Blue Aragonite

Calm and Emotional Healing

Blue Aragonite is a calming crystal that promotes emotional healing and a sense of calm. It helps you release emotional pain and trauma, supporting overall well-being. Blue Aragonite is often used for relaxation and stress relief.

"I am emotionally healed, calm, and stress-free in every moment."

Find locations: Spain, Mexico, United States

Uvarovite

Abundance and Connection

Uvarovite is a crystal associated with abundance and connection. It helps you attract prosperity and fosters a deep connection with the Earth. Uvarovite also enhances a sense of gratitude and appreciation.

"I am open to the flow of abundance, and I am deeply connected to the Earth"

Find locations: Russia, Finland, Turkey

Larimar

Calm and Serenity

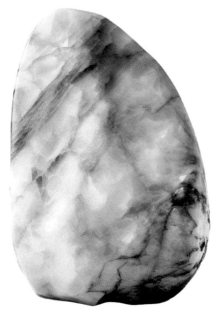

Larimar is a calming crystal that promotes serenity and inner peace. It is often associated with the energies of the ocean and helps you release stress and find tranquility. Larimar also enhances clear communication.

"I am calm, at peace, and stress-free in every moment."

Find locations: Dominican Republic

Larvikite

Protection and Inner Power

Larvikite is a crystal of protection and inner power. It helps in shielding your energy from negative influences and enhances inner strength. Larvikite is often used for grounding and personal growth.

"I am protected and in tune with my inner power"

Find locations: Norway, Canada

Yellow Calcite

Joy and Self-confidence

Yellow Calcite is a crystal of joy and self-confidence. It enhances positivity and helps boost self-esteem. Yellow Calcite is also associated with the solar plexus chakra, promoting personal power and vitality.

"I am joyful, confident, and I embrace my personal power"

Find locations: Mexico, United States

Apophyllite

Spiritual Connection and Clarity

Apophyllite is a crystal that enhances spiritual connection and clarity. It helps you connect with higher realms and promotes inner peace. Apophyllite is often used for meditation and spiritual work.

"I am connected to the divine, and my mind is clear and focused."

Find locations: India, Brazil, Germany

89

Black Moonstone

Transformation, Intuition

Black Moonstone is a stone of transformation and intuition. It enhances one's psychic abilities and helps in understanding and embracing change. It is often used for protection and grounding during transitional periods.

"I embrace change with grace and intuition."

Find locations: India, United States, Madagascar

Dalmatian Jasper

Joy, Playfulness

Dalmatian Jasper is a stone that brings joy and playfulness into life. It's believed to counteract negative emotions and encourage positivity. It also enhances one's sense of humor and creative expression.

"I find joy and playfulness in every moment."

Find locations: Mexico, Brazil, United States

Yellow Malachite

Inner Power, Self-Confidence

Yellow Malachite is a stone of inner power and self-confidence. It helps in unlocking one's potential, fostering self-belief, and promoting personal growth. This crystal is associated with the solar plexus chakra and self-empowerment.

"I radiate self-confidence and inner power."

Find locations: Democratic Republic of the Congo

Orange Aventurine

Creativity, Prosperity

Orange Aventurine is a crystal that stimulates creativity and attracts prosperity. It is often used to boost one's self-esteem and motivation. This stone brings a sense of abundance and optimism to one's life.

"I embrace my creative potential and attract abundance."

Find locations: India, Brazil, Russia

Mangano Calcite

Compassion, Emotional Healing

Mangano Calcite is known for its gentle and soothing energy that promotes emotional healing and compassion. It is used to release past traumas and promote self-love and forgiveness.

"I am open to healing, compassion, and self-love."

Find locations: Peru, Poland, Pakistan

Sulfur

Purification, Energy

Sulfur is a mineral known for its purifying and energizing properties. It is used to clear negative energies and promote vitality and stamina. This crystal is associated with the element of fire.

"I purify my energy and embrace vitality."

Find locations: Italy, United States, Japan

Tsavorite Garnet

Abundance, Prosperity

Tsavorite Garnet is a stone that attracts abundance and prosperity. It is believed to enhance one's financial success and stimulate the heart chakra. This crystal brings a sense of joy and well-being.

"I welcome abundance and prosperity into my life."

Find locations: Kenya, Tanzania, Madagascar

Yellow Apatite

Clarity, Confidence

Yellow Apatite is a crystal that promotes mental clarity and self-confidence. It helps in setting clear goals, improving focus, and boosting self-esteem. It's associated with the solar plexus chakra.

"I am confident, focused, and clear in my intentions."

Find locations: Mexico, Canada, Russia

Red Chalcedony

Vitality, Motivation

Red Chalcedony is a stone that enhances vitality and motivation. It is often used to increase physical energy, stamina, and courage. This crystal is believed to stimulate creativity and passion.

"I am filled with vitality and motivation."

Find locations: United States, India, Brazil

K2 Stone

Enlightenment, Insight

K2 Stone is known for its connection to higher consciousness and providing insights. It combines Azurite and Granite, bringing wisdom, clarity, and a deep sense of inner peace.

"I open myself to enlightenment and inner wisdom."

Find locations: Pakistan

Bloodstone

Healing, Strength

Bloodstone is a powerful healing crystal that enhances physical strength and endurance. It is often used for purifying the blood and promoting courage. This stone is associated with vitality and renewal.

"I am strong and filled with healing energy."

Find locations: India, Brazil, Australia

Indigo Gabbro

Transformation, Intuition

Indigo Gabbro is a crystal that aids in personal transformation and enhances intuition. It helps in accessing deeper insights and spiritual growth. This stone is also known as "Mystic Merlinite."

"I trust my intuition and embrace transformation."

Find locations: Madagascar, United States

Malachite Azurite

Inner Wisdom, Balance

Malachite Azurite combines the properties of Malachite and Azurite. It promotes inner wisdom, balance, and spiritual growth. It's a stone of transformation and insight.

"I find balance and wisdom within myself."

Find locations: Russia, Australia, Congo

INDEX SORTED BY CRYSTAL NAME

INDEX SORTED BY CRYSTAL MEANING

Made in the USA
Las Vegas, NV
06 February 2024

85392605R00064